THE BALVIHAR BOOK OF JOKES — 2

Cartoons by
Bharati Sukhatankar

CENTRAL CHINMAYA MISSION TRUST
MUMBAI - 400 072

© **Central Chinmaya Mission Trust**

First Edition	December	- 2003	- 3,000 copies
Reprint	September	- 2004	- 3,000 copies
Reprint	July	- 2006	- 3,000 copies
Reprint	February	- 2009	- 3,000 copies

Published by:
Central Chinmaya Mission Trust
Sandeepany Sadhanalaya
Saki Vihar Road,
Mumbai-400 072. India,
Tel.: 091-22-2857 2367, 2857 5806
Fax : 091-22-2857 3065
Email :ccmt@chinmayamission.com
Website: www.chinmayamission.com

Distribution Centre in USA:
Chinmaya Mission West
Publications Dicision
560 Bridgetown Pike,
Langhorne, PA 19053, USA
Tel.: (215) 396-0390
Fax: (215) 396-9710
www. chinmayapublicatons.org
publications@chinmaya.org

Printed by:
JAK Printers Pvt. Ltd.,
JAK Compound,
Dadoji Konddeo Cross Lane,
Off. Dr. Babasaheb Ambedkar Marg,
Byculla (East), Mumbai - 400 027.
Tel.: 2377 2222 Telefax: 2377 1212
Email: jakprint@vsnl.com

Price: Rs. 100.00

ISBN: 978-81-7597-206-3

Foreword

The Bal Vihar magazine has played a vital role in the history of the Chinmaya Mission. Started in 1969 by Pujya Gurudev Swami Chinmayananda it was aimed at moulding the minds of the children and thereby laying the foundation for producing men and women of strong moral character, upholding the timeless values of Indian culture. Pujya Gurudev's idea was to "catch them young."

Towards this goal, Bal Vihar has worked for over thirty years. Much valuable material has been published so far and so it was dicided that in this, the 50th year of the Chinmaya Movement, it would be a good idea to reprint a series of all-colour Bal Vihar books under different titles. This would strengthen the grass root level activities and help the Bal Vihar children and sevaks.

I commend the work done by the Bal Vihar team and wish them all success in their ongoing efforts.

Mumbai

December 2001

Swami Tejomayanada

Editor's Note

Laughter is what sets apart man from other creatures. The ability to see the lighter side of life, to smile when the going gets tough, to laugh at one's own idiosyncracies and follies - this makes life joyous.

This is Bal Vihar's tribute to Gurudev Swami Chinmayananda's spirit of fun and laughter.

(Brni. Vividisha Chaitanya)

Mumbai

December 2003

1.   *Hemu :* Mom, can I have one rupee for an old man crying outside on the street?
Mom : Yes dear, but what is the man crying about?
Hemu : "Ice-cream -- one rupee each!"

2.   *Mother :* Rupa, I had kept two chocolates in this cupboard. One of them is missing.
Rupa : It was dark, mom, so I must have missed the second chocolate.

1

3. *Pappu :* Papa, can you write in the dark?
Papa : Yes, I think so. What do you want me to write?
Pappu : Your signature on my report card.

4. *Mom :* Did you eat all the cookies?
Tinku : I did not touch a single one.
Mom : That is funny. There is only one cookie left.
Tinku : That is the one I did not touch.

5.   *Mother :* Do you remember you promised to behave properly? And if you didn't, I promised to whack you? Well, you have behaved very badly today.
Meena : But since I didn't keep my promise, you needn't keep yours.

6.   *Son :* Dad, how much am I worth to you?
Father : O, more than a million, son.
Son : In that case, can you advance me 5% of it?

7. *Pappu :* Mummy, have I descended from a monkey?
Mummy : I wouldn't know, dear. I have never met your father's people.

8. *Pintoo :* I eaten 7 chapatis for lunch, mom.
Mom : Ate, Pintoo, ate.
Pintoo : No mom, seven. There were eight on the plate but I couldn't eat the last one.

9. *Father :* If I have twelve apples and I give away
seven, how many will I have left?
Meenu : I don't know. In my school, we do arithmetic with
oranges only.

10.   *Mithu :* You won't believe this -- I got two ice-cream cones for nothing.
Mother : How did that happen?
Mithu : I had a cone in each hand and asked the sales lady to take the money out of my pants pocket, but to be careful and not disturb the mice.

11.   One day when Dad came home from work, he was surprised to see Tony writing on their pet dog, Snowy.
Dad : Good heavens! What on earth are you doing?
Tony : Teacher asked us to write an essay on our pet. So that's what I'm doing.

12. *Mohit :* When can I have a younger brother or sister?
Mom : Why, what is your hurry?
Mohit : Well, how long can I blame the pup?

13. *Mother :* Are you sure you washed the salad properly?
Gauri : Of course I did – I even used soap!

14. *Daddy :* Where do you want to go this summer?
    Neel : Somewhere I haven't been for a long time.
    Daddy : How about the barbershop?

15. *Ravi :* Dad, I think our neighbour has no feeling for music.
Dad : What makes you think so?
Ravi : Well, he told me to cut open my drums and see what's inside!

16. *Dad :* This money which you have received to buy sweets, save it and put it in your piggy bank.
    Renu : Sure, then you can give me more money to buy sweets.

17. *Priya :* Mom, may I go out and play with my friend Manoj?
    Mom : No, I don't like your friend Manoj.
    Priya : Then may I go out and have a fight with him?

18. *Pavan :* I am not feeling well. I think I won't go to school today.
Mother : Where do you not feel well? In your head? Your stomach?
Pavan : In school.

19. *Ronnie to Dad :* Bobby just called -- his Dad wants to copy my homework when you have finished doing it.

20. *Pinky :* Aunty Pam kissed me today.
Mom : Really? And did you kiss her back?
Pinky : Of course not. I kissed her face.

21. *Rita :* Why is your hair white in between, mom?
Mom : My hair turns white when you trouble me.
Rita : O, dear. Then you must have really troubled
grandma -- her head is completely white.

22. *Pavan :* I am not going to school anymore.
Father : Why Pavan?
Pavan : It's a sheer waste of time. I cannot read, I
cannot write and they won't let me talk.

23. *Monu :* Hey, mom. Do you know any circus tricks?
Mom : No, I don't.
Monu : Then why did the lady next door say that you
make Dad dance on your fingertips?

24. *Son :* Dad, is a thousand rupees a lot of money?
Dad : Well, it depends whether you are earning it or
spending it.

25. *Father looking at report card :* Pankaj, these grades
are unacceptable.
Pankaj : I agree with you, Dad. Let us tell the teacher.

26. *Father :* You have failed! Aren't you ashamed of yourself?
Son : But father, I have the highest marks among those who failed.

27. *Dad :* How was your English exam today?
Suneeta : It was fine. Teacher asked us to hand in a neat paper -- so I did not write anything on it.

28. *College student :* I really would like to have a car, dad.
Father : A car, you say? Then what will you do with the two feet that God has given you?
College student : I will put one on the accelerator and the other on the brake!

29. Father tries to teach his son how to swim. After a while - *Son :* Dad, can we stop now? I have had enough water to drink.

30.　*Babloo :* Papa, please don't do my homework today. Let mummy do it.
Father : Why?
Babloo : Because when teacher saw the homework you had done for me yesterday, she called me a donkey.

31.　*Father :* Well, what question were you asked in the exam today?
Son : What is the thing you don't like at all?
Father : And what did you write?
Son : Nothing. I just pasted the question paper on the answer sheet.

32.　*Mom :* How were the exam questions?
Sarika : They were easy, but I had trouble with the answers.

33.　*Raj :* Dad, will you please buy me a harmonium?
Dad : On one condition -- you must not disturb me.
Raj : It's a deal -- I will only play it when you are sleeping.

34.　*Father :* How many of your answers were wrong?
Son : One.
Father : Only one? What about the other nine? Were they correct?
Son : The other nine? O, I didn't write those answers at all!

35. *Dad :* Mala, go and get the hammer from the neighbour - I have to drive nails in the wall.
Mala : Dad, the neighbour says he doesn't have a hammer.
Dad : How miserly he is. He has a hammer and won't give it. Never mind. Climb the ladder and get our own hammer down from the loft.

37. "Darling", the mother asked her small boy, "Why are you making faces at your new bulldog?"
"Well", the child defended himself, "He started it!"

38. *Father :* I can't understand why you don't do better in Mathematics. It was my favourite subject and I was always first in class.
Sandhya : But Dad, I did get 7 out of 10 sums correct.
Father : That's OK. But 90% is not good enough now a days.

39. *Father :* Always remember, son, that charity begins at home.
Son : Okay Dad. Now please give me two rupees.

40. *Radha :* Mummy, I think our neighbours are very poor.
Mother : Why do you think so?
Radha : Because they made such a big fuss today when the baby swallowed a 25 paise coin!

41. *Mother :* Raghu, if your bed is tidy tomorrow morning, I will give you a tenner for ice-cream.
Next morning, mother is surprised to see a neat and tidy bed.
Mother : I can't believe it. How did you manage it, Raghu?
Raghu : Simple. I slept on the floor last night.

42. *Mother :* How many sums did teacher give in the test today?
Manoj : Five
Mother : And did you get them all right?
Manoj : Except the first two... and the last three.

43. *Father :* You should really be ashamed of yourself. See how many certificates your sister has got, whether in academics or on the sports field.
Son : But dad, I too, have got one certificate.
Father : Which one?
Son : My birth certificate.

44. *Tommy :* Stop beating me, mom, have you not got a tongue?
Mom : Yes, but my arms are longer.

45. *Father :* Mini, why are you late from school?
Mini : I was in detention.
Father : Why?
Mini : Because I answered a question.
Father : What question?
Mini : Who put the ink in the glue?

46. *Son :* My teacher knows you helped me with my homework.
Father : How?
Son : She said one person alone couldn't make so many mistakes.

47. *Mom :* Look here, Girish. You must always play with clever and intelligent kids.
Girish : That's not possible, mom.
Mom : Why not?
Girish : Because their moms also tell them the same thing.

48. *Mother :* Now look here, Ravi — there is a ghost in the cupboard where I keep the cake.
Ravi : Really? Then how come you never blame the ghost when a piece of cake is missing?

49. *Father :* How many questions you ask! I wonder what would have happened if I had asked so many questions as a little boy.
Babloo : Perhaps you would have been able to answer some of mine?

50. *Sonu :* Mom, come soon! I have just knocked down the ladder.
Mom : I am busy in the kitchen -- go and tell dad.
Sonu : He already knows it - he is hanging from the roof.

51. *Mother* : Son, it is high time you got married. I will get the most beautiful girl for you -- then you will live happily ever after.
Son : To tell you the truth, when I see Dad washing the dishes and clothes, I just do not have the courage to get married.

52. *Mother* : Why are you crying?
Jai : Teacher asked me to get out of the class today.
Mother : I am sure you were creating a din -- now tell me the truth.
Jai : No, I promise I wasn't creating a din. I was sleeping.

53. *Pappu* : Mummy, is red ink very expensive?
Mummy : Not at all son. Why do you ask?
Pappu : I spilt some on Daddy's pants and he was very annoyed.

54. *Mother to Gopi* : These are two coins – with one rupee buy some peanuts and with the other buy a lemon.
After a while, Gopi returns empty handed.
Mother : Where are the peanuts and the lemon?
Gopi : You forgot to tell me with which coin to buy the peanuts and with which the lemon.

17

55. A miserly father bought a pair of specs for his son.
The son wore the specs and sat at his study table.
Father : Are you reading?
Son : No.
Father : Are you writing, then?
Son : No.
Father : Then why are you using the specs unnecessarily?
Remove them and keep them aside.

56. *Meena (at the dining table) :* Papa, do we also eat insects with our food?
Papa: What silly questions you ask. We'll talk about this after dinner.
And then after dinner-
Papa : Yes, now what were you asking me?
Meena : It's not important any more. There were two insects in your vegetable at dinner time.

57. *Son :* Dad, I just saved you some money.
Dad : How's that?
Son : I won't need new books next year – I am staying in the same class again.

58. *Mom :* Eat your spinach, dear, it makes your teeth strong.
Meena : Why don't you give some to grandpa?

59. *Wife to husband :* A terrible thing happened today. I was ironing your shirts and the blue one got burnt.
Husband : Never mind. I have another identical blue shirt.
Wife : I know – I cut a piece from it and patched up the burnt shirt.

60. *Wife :* What's today's date?
Husband : I don't know.
Wife : But you are reading the newspaper.
Husband : That won't help. It's yesterday's paper.

61. *Newly-wed wife :* O dear, I think there is too much salt in the soup.
Husband : Not at all, dear. But perhaps there is not enough soup for the salt.

62. *Wife :* (on a vacation) O my God! I forgot to turn off the gas burner before we left.
Husband : Don't worry, dear. I forgot to turn off the tap in the bathroom.

63. *Absent minded professor, writing a letter :* It was on the tip of my tongue! It was on the tip of my tongue!
Wife : Since it was on the tip of your tongue, it will come back. Meanwhile, why don't you write the next sentence?
Professor : I am not talking about the sentence. I am talking about the postage stamp.

64. *Young Lady :* How quickly can I learn German?
German Teacher : That depends upon you. But why are you in such a hurry?
Young Lady : We have just adopted a six month old German baby and we are not able to understand what he says.

65. *Wife to husband :* I have been watching you for the last few days. You bring home stacks of medicine every day. What exactly is your ailment?
Husband : Nothing. Our chemist tenant has not paid rent for 3 months.

66. *Wife to absent-minded husband :* Have you noticed? Our baby has started walking.
Husband : Really? Since when?
Wife : Since a week.
Husband : O, then he must have walked quite far by now.

67. *Wife to husband, who has returned from the barber :* Good heavens! What a haircut! What on earth made you have it cut so short?
Husband : The barber didn't have change for five rupees. So I told him to cut another five rupees worth of hair.

68. *Mini :* We have been married for 20 years and we have never quarrelled even once.
Rini : Really? How is that?
Mini : When I am in the mood to fight, my husband folds his hands and says sorry.
Rini : And if he is in the mood to fight?
Mini : O, that has never happened.

69. *Husband :* We have been married for six years and we have not agreed on a single thing.
Wife : Not six – we have been married for seven years.

70. *Miser to wife :* Let's eat out today.
Wife : How nice. Which restaurant shall we go to?
Miser : Who said anything about restaurant? There is a beautiful moon outside – let's eat in the backyard.

71.   Junior went to spend his vacation with his grandparents on the farm. When he returned, his mother asked, "Did you have a good time?"
Junior : No. It was most boring. Grandpa and Grandma sat around all day with nothing on.
Mother was agahst : Nothing on !
Junior : No. They had nothing on – no TV, no radio, not even a computer.

72.   *Bipin :* I heard that your wife is missing – I hope you have lodged a complaint with the police.
Nikhil : No, I haven't.
Bipin : Why not?
Nikhil : Because last time she went missing and I lodged a complaint, they brought her back.

73.   *Mohan :* How did the quarrel with your wife end last night?
Sohan : Well, she was down on her knees.
Mohan : Really sorry, was she?
Sohan : Well... actually that was the only way she could get me out from under the bed.

74.   Angry wife playing cards with her husband : "You cannot play a friendly little game – no, you always have to try to win!"

75.   Wife : What will you do if I die?
Husband : I'll go crazy.
Wife : You won't remarry?
Husband : A crazy man can do anything.

76.   Wife : Why do you always go out into the balcony when I sing? Don't you like to hear me?
Husband : It isn't that, dear. I just don't want the neighbours to think that I am beating you.

77.   Husband : Why are you after me to look for a new house? You were perfectly happy with it when we came to live here.
Wife : Sheesh. But of course this is a nice house. It's just that I am tired of fighting with the same neighbours for the last three years.

78.   Billy : I must rush home, otherwise my wife will sit around without eating.
Bunty : Lucky guy! Your wife waits to eat with you.
Billy : Wait nothing. I must first go and cook the food!

79. Wife returning from shopping : See what a huge cloth I have brought to stitch you a handkerchief.
Husband : It is really huge, but how can I use a six metre handkerchief?
Wife : O, don't worry. I will stitch a salwar kameez from the cloth that remains after stitching your handkerchief.

80. Ramesh : So, did you have a good time on your birthday?
Suresh : No. I had made up my mind to stay at home and my wife had made up her face to go out.

81. Sunny : Where are you going?
Bunny : To the Chemist's. My mother has a headache and I am going to get her some aspirin.
Sunny : I don't think there is any need for that – with you out of the house, her headache must have disappeared.

82. Twinkle : Hey, why don't you girls come over to my house? I will give you a treat for the New Year.
Bubble : (Groan) Not today. We have just had a feast at Dimple's house.
Twinkle : That's even better – then you won't eat so many of my cakes and sweets.

26

83. *Ramu :* I found 50 paise on the road today.
Shamu : O, that's mine. I lost a 50 paise coin today.
Ramu : But what I found was two 25 paise coins.
Shamu : That's right. My 50 paise coin broke in two when it fell.

84. *Bunty :* Come along Sunny, we are getting late. Are you ready for school?
Sunny : Sure I am ready. My bag is packed, my books are in, my compass box is in, my pencils are sharpened, my shoes are polished, my hair is combed. I have had my breakfast... but there's one thing I haven't done.
Bunty : What's that?
Sunny : My homework.

85. *Ram Prasad :* I can't go to work today – my car is in the repair shop.
Shiv Prasad : Then take a bus.
Ram Prasad : I can't, it's too big for my garage.

86. *Billu :* When does a person become middle-aged?
Tillu : When he stops growing upwards and starts growing in the middle.

87. *Dolly :* I am putting on too much weight. What should I do?
Lolly : Push yourself away from the dining table, three times a day.

88. *Pramod :* If I saw a man beating a donkey and I stopped him, which virtue would I be practising?
Vinod : Brotherly love!

89. *Ajit :* Know what? I gazed at a tiger's eyes for full 10 minutes today.
Ranjit : Gosh! Weren't you scared? Then what happened?
Ajit : Nothing. The shopkeeper said either buy the toy or leave the shop.

90. *Anu :* Can you stand on your head?
Sonu : No, it's too high.

91. *Meera :* Why do you part your hair in the middle?
Lalita : So that my head will be evenly balanced.

92. *Rex :* If you pull the right leg of my parrot, it says, "Welcome". If you pull the left leg, it says, "Thank you".
Tex : Suppose, I pull both legs, what will it say?
Rex : I don't know.
Parrot : I'll say, "Watch out, you fool, I'll fall!"

93. *Mohan :* If you found a hundred rupee note, would you keep it?
Ramesh : No.
Mohan : That is a good boy. What would you do with it?
Ramesh : I would spend it.

94. *Jimmy :* I have been thinking, and I have come to the conclusion that we must not ask our parents so many questions.
Timmy : And why is that?
Jimmy : Because asking too many questions will expose their ignorance!

95. *Sarita :* My husband is very careless – he is constantly losing the buttons on his shirt.
Kavita : May be they are not sewn on properly.
Sarita : Could be. He is not very good at sewing either.

96. *Ajit :* Are you excercising to lose weight?
Sujit : Of course I am – I go horse-riding every day.
Ajit : Really? And has it made a difference?
Sujit : Sure. The horse has really become thin.

97. *Pradeep :* You are a fool! A donkey! A monkey! An idiot!
Sandeep : Be careful what you are saying. I am warning you – your face may just come and dash on my fist.

98. *Ravi :* My father shaves twice a day.
Shyam : That is nothing, my father shaves 40 to 60 times a day.
Ravi : That is impossible. Does his beard grow every minute?
Shyam : No, he is a barber.

99.   *Anil :* My father is a great musician. When he plays the veena, hundreds of people stand still, spell-bound.
Sunil : When my father plays his instrument, thousands of people leave their work and head for home.
Anil : Really? That's wonderful. What does he play?
Sunil : The siren in the mill.

100. *Raj :* How did you burn your hand?
Taj : I put it in hot water.
Raj : Stupid! You should have felt the water before doing that.

101. *Tarun :* The exams are over. Have you made a list of holiday activities?
Arun : Yes. I have – and we must have the maximum fun before the results are out!

102. *Pinku :* What is the best way to avoid a road accident?
Smart Alec : Travel by train.

103. *Lucy :* I spent last summer in a very pretty place in Switzerland.
Rosy : Berne?
Lucy : No, I almost froze.

104. *Mohit :* All extremely bright people are conceited.
Rohit : O, I don't know – I am not.

105. *Rohini :* I got an 'A' in spelling.
Mohini : You are a dope. There is no'A' in 'Spelling'.

106. *Mohan :* What do you call a person who paints a car?
Sohan : Car-painter!

107. Amit : Hey, what has happened to your hand?
Sumit : We had a question for home work – how many teeth does a cow have? I put my hand in the cow's mouth to count her teeth and she clamped her mouth to count my fingers.

108. Usha : When your baby cries at night, who gets up?
Asha : The whole neighbourhood.

109. Raghu to bald friend : How did you lose your hair?
Bald man : Worry.
Raghu : What did you worry about?
Bald man : About losing my hair.

110. Gopu : What does your father do?
Deepu : He sells furniture.
Gopu : Is his business doing well?
Deepu : O yes, we have only one bed left.

113. Rohit : Why does the hair on your head turn white before the hair in your beard?
Rahul : Beacuse it is 15 years older than the hair in your beard.

114. Bunty : I have three pairs of spectacles.
Bubble : Really? What do you do with three pairs?
Bunty : One is for long sight, one is for short sight, and the third one is to look for the other two.

115. *Seema :* What is more useful after it is broken?
Reema : I don't know. You tell.
Seema : An egg.

116. *Rina :* I hit my thumb with the hammer.
Mina : How did that happen?
Rina : I was aiming at a nail.

117. *Meenu :* Why are you jumping on the potato patch?
Teenu : I want mashed potatoes.

118. *Mohan :* I am in deep trouble. Every hair on my
head is under debt. Tell me, what should I do?
Ramesh : Simple. Just shave off your head!

119. *Gaurav :* Please lend me a hundred rupees. I will
return it as soon as I reach Calcutta.
Saurav : When are you going to Calcutta?
Gaurav : For heaven's sake, who is going to Calcutta?

120. *Big Brother :* Tchah! Why are you always so dirty?
Little Brother : Perhaps it's because I'm a lot closer to the
ground than you are.

121. *Sunder :* I am going to give you a book for your
birthday.
Shyam : Thanks, but I already have one.

122. *Rakesh :* When water becomes ice, what is the change that takes place?
Ashish : The price, madam.

123. *Jeevan :* Why are you wearing two wrist watches? Isn't one good enough?
Pavan : No. One watch has only the minute hand, the other has only the hour hand. So I need both, you see.

124. *Mohan Rao :* I will have to get a new denture made – I have lost one tooth in my denture.
Shyam Rao : For the sake of one tooth, will you get a whole new denture made?
Mohan Rao : Yes, I will have to. It was the last tooth in my denture.

125. *Anil :* He has been sitting there all day, wasting his time, doing nothing.
Sunil : How do you know?
Anil : I know. I have been watching him all the time.

126. *Sonu :* If I throw a peanut to an elephant, why won't he eat it?
Monu : I don't know.
Sonu : Because the peanut is made of plastic. Okay. If I throw a real peanut, why won't the elephant eat it?
Monu : I don't know.
Sonu : Because the elephant is made of plastic!

127. *Pat :* I finally finished that jigsaw puzzle.
Tom : Did it take long?
Pat : The packet said 2-4 years, but I finished it in 6 months.

128. *Gopu :* My uncle is a man of letters.
Dopu : Really? That's great.
Gopu : Yeah. He works at the post office.

129. *Jingo :* My father is a real brave lion. He also has eagle eyes and is as strong as an elephant.
Ringo : Really? How much do you charge to see him?
Jingo : O, we don't charge our kith and kin anything.

130. *Meena (indulging in self-pity) :* Nobody loves me. Nobody understands me. The whole world hates me.
Mohit (her brother) : That's not true, Meena. Many people don't even know you.

131. Aruna : Manisha hasn't come to school for the last two days. What's the matter with her?
Karuna : Do you see those four steps?
Aruna : Yes, I do.
Karuna : Well, she didn't.

132. Sonali : You look really foolish to me with those thick lens glasses.
Rupali : Yeah, but if I remove them, you will look foolish to me.

133. Sujit : How many seconds are there in a year?
Ajit : Gosh, I don't know. You tell me.
Sujit : Twelve - 2nd of Jan, 2nd of Feb, 2nd of March .....

134. *Billu :* Is it bad luck to have a black cat follow you?
Tillu : That depends on whether you are a man or a mouse.

135. *Amit :* Your pup just bit my ankle.
Sumit : Well, you don't expect such a little dog to bite your neck, do you?

136. *Beena :* Yesterday I saw my nephew for the first time – he is rather small, has a fat belly, no hair and he drinks all the time.
Reeta : (Gasp!) For heaven's sake, how old is he?
Beena : Three months!

137. *Bhaloo :* What will you do when you are as big as your father?
Laloo : Diet.

138. *Pintoo :* What is it – Mama has them, Papa has them, but we don't.
Chintoo : Can't think – you tell me.
Pintoo : Children!

139. Girish : I just saved the life of a beggar.
Ashish : You did? How?
Girish : Well, I asked him what he would do if I gave him a fifty rupee note. And he said that he would die of happiness. I saved his life by not giving him the note!

140. Manoj : If you see a man opening the door of his car for his wife, what would you think?
Sanjay : Either his car is new or his wife is new.

141. Shiv : What are the seasons in your country?
Jeff : You mean here, in the USA?
Shiv : Yes, of course.
Jeff : Baseball, Football, Basketball and vacation.

142. Sudhir : Yesterday, I saw a man beating a woman in the middle of the road. So I went and said to him, "If you have guts, why don't you beat a man instead of a woman?"
Sumant : Then what happened?
Sudhir : I don't know. When I opened my eyes, I was in the hospital.

143. *Gaurav :* My father was very strong when he
was small.
Saurav : How do you know?
Gaurav : Grandfather says that whenever father used to cry,
he used to raise the rooftop!

144. *Sheela :* I hear you bought a dachshund.
Leela : Yes, we did — so that all the children can pet him at
the same time.

146. *Gappu :* Which dog has no tail?
Tappu : I don't know. You tell me.
Gappu: A hot dog.

147. *Suresh :* Man always gets pain in the weakest part of his body.
Mahesh : That's it! That explains why you have such frequent headaches.

148. *Arun :* I have changed my job – in the old job the noise was awful.
Varun : What are you doing now?
Arun : I am in construction work, pile driving.
Varun : O, this noise must be terrible too. What were you doing before?
Arun : Driving a school bus!

149. *Sachin :* I was just thinking – how much will it cost to take a trip to Paris and back?
Nitin : Nothing.
Sachin : Nothing? How's that?
Nitin : Well, if you are just thinking, it won't cost you anything.

150. *Dimple :* Last week you had bought some medicine to improve your memory. Has it made a difference?
Simple : I cannot say anything just yet – I forget to take it every evening.

151. Two friends at the movie.
"Can you see the picture?"
"Yes".
"Is your seat OK?"
"Yes".
"Are you confortable?"
"Yes".
"Can we change seats?"

152. *Gappu :* I don't understand grown-ups at all.
Tappu : Why, what happened?
Gappu : Well, if I talk, my parents tell me to keep quiet. And if I keep quiet, they take my temperature.

153. *Rohan :* A man lost in the desert finally came across a house. But all it had was a bed and a calendar.
Mohan : Gosh! How did he survive?
Rohan : He drank water from the bed springs and ate the dates of the calendar.

154. *First friend :* Why are you so sad today?
Second friend : I had a fight with my wife and she said she wouldn't talk to me for a full week.
First friend : Ah, and that makes you sad?
Second friend : No. Today is the last day of the week.

155. *Bob :* Will you be using your pick-axe and shovel today?
Tom thinks, "He is always borrowing things from me. Today, I'll teach him a lesson".
Tom : O yes. I will be working in the garden and using them from morning till evening.
Bob : O good. Then I can borrow your car as I have to go out today.

46

156. *Shiv :* Why do you eat two grapefruits every day?
Gopi : It cleans the body.
Shiv : It does? Well, I would rather take a shower.

157. *Boy to constable :* Come quick. My father and a neighbour have been fighting for the last half an hour and the neighbour is beating up my father.
Constable : Fighting for half an hour! Why didn't you call me earlier?
Boy : Because earlier my father was beating him up.

158. Constable : Did you rob this man?
Thief : Yes.
Constable : Now put everything belonging to this man on the table.
Thief does so, but keeps back a watch.
Constable : What about that watch?
Thief : O, that. That I robbed from another man.

159. Lawyer : Did you consult any other lawyer before you brought your case here?
Client : Yes, I did.
Lawyer : And what did he tell you?
Client : He told me that I need not go to him – that any third-rate lawyer could handle it.

160. *Constable :* Dogs are not allowed in the park. Is this your dog?
Vishal : No sir, it is not mine.
Constable : But it is following you.
Vishal : You also, are following me.

161. Judge to accused : And remember, you must never insult a policeman by calling him an ass.
Accused : O, I didn't know that. But is it OK if I call an ass a policeman?
Judge : That you may, if it gives you satisfaction.
Accused turning to the policeman, who had arrested him: Good day, policeman.

162. Pickpocket, boasting to friend : Nobody on earth has picked my pocket yet.
Friend (smugly) : O, but it will be picked quite soon, don't worry.
Pickpocket : Really? When?
Friend : The day you get married.

163. Judge to woman seeking divorce : And why do you feel that your husband is tired of you and neglects you?
Woman : Because he hasn't come home a single day in the past five years.

164. A lawyer wanted to trick a peasant.
So he asked him : Do you know how to read and write?
Peasant : I can write, but I can't read.
Lawyer : OK, Write here, "I owe this man Rs.500".
The peasant wrote something on the paper.
Lawyer : What have you written? These are just scribbles.
Peasant : How do I know what I've written – I told you I cannot read.

165. *Prison Director :* So you want to be a prison guard.
Sometimes the prisoners become very difficult – are you
sure you will be able to handle them?
Applicant : Of course I am sure. Anybody who doesn't
behave will get thrown out!

166. *Police Officer, writing down complaint :* When you
entered the house and saw all your belongings scattered,
why did you not call us immediately?
Housewife : That is because I thought my husband had
been looking for his tie.

167. There was a car accident. The driver and his lawyer discussed implications.
Lawyer : It will be difficult to plead "Not Guilty". You will have to prove that the bicyclist you injured had a speed of 100km/h and the cat coming from the left prevented you from seeing him!

168. Lawyer, cross-examining the witness : You say you are an illiterate woman. How is it that you are answering all my questions so well?
Witness : I don't think one has to be literate to answer stupid questions.

169. *Lawyer :* You say you were 100 feet away from the scene of the accident. Now will you please tell the court how far you can see clearly?
Witness : Well, when I get up in the morning, I can see the sun and people say it is 93 million miles away.

170. *Prosecutor :* This crime was the work of a master criminal! It was carried out in a skilfully clever manner.
Defendant : Flattery will get you nowhere! I am not going to confess!

171. *Lawyer :* Have you got enough cash with you for paying my fee?
Thief : No. I am sorry. I do not have any cash, but I have a new Mercedes car.
Lawyer : All right, that is fine. I will take your case. Now, tell me what is the charge against you?
Thief : Stealing a new Mercedes Car.

172. *Judge :* You picked this man's pocket in broad daylight. How come he never came to know?
Culprit : Excuse me, your honour. But it will cost you Rs.500 - to learn this from me.

173. *Judge :* Why did you park your car there?
Accused : Because the sign said, "Fine for parking".

174. *Judge :* Have you ever been up before me?
Accused : I wouldn't know – what time do you get up?

175. *Judge :* You carried out all these robberies on your own, you say. Don't you have an accomplice?
Accused : Alas, I had to carry out these robberies all alone – where can you get an honest accomplice these days?

176. *Judge :* Why did you raid the same shop twice?
Offender : Well, my wife did not like the dresses I had stolen the first time so I had to go back to change them.

177. *Client :* My case is so complicated that I need a really old, experienced lawyer to represent it in court.
Young Lawyer : Sir, please keep on talking about it – I am sure to be old and experienced by the time you finish.

178. *Judge :* Do you know where you'll go if you tell a lie?
Accused : To hell.
Judge : And if you tell the truth?
Accused : Straight to jail.

179. First Prisoner : I have noticed that your relatives never come to visit you. Why is that?
Second Prisoner : O, that's because there is no need – they are all inmates of this prison.

180. Judge : Ten witnesses have said that they saw you stealing the car. What do you have to say to that?
Accused : Just this – there are thousands of people who didn't see me steal the car.

181. Judge : You are accused of having run away from your wife. What is your defence?
Accused : If I could have defended myself, your honour, would I have had to run away?

182. Judge : You have been a good prisoner. So I will allow you to choose your mode of death.
Prisoner (hopefully) : How about death by old age and natural causes?

183. *Policeman :* Madam, did you see the number of the car that knocked you down?
Lady : No – but the lady was wearing a red kanjeevaram sari with a black border and had fake diamonds in her ears.

184. *Judge to accused :* How many times have you appeared in this court! Aren't you ashamed of yourself?
Accused : I come here once in a while, your Honour. But you come to court every day....

185. *Traffic Cop :* Here, stop your car. What's your name?
Speeding girl : O, mine's Mona. What's yours?

186. *Two-wheeler rider :* Why have you stopped me? I was not driving very fast.
Traffic cop : I have stopped you because your wife has fallen off the pillion at the last turning.

187. *New visitor in town to constable :* Why do you have so many 'DRIVE SLOW' signs here?
Constable : Because there is no hospital nearby.

188. A lady had a car accident. At the repair shop she asked, "Won't take long, will it? Just some minor repairs?"
Mechanic : Sure thing. We will just have to put a new car on the licence plate!

189. *First man :* Today, I lost control over my car.
Second man : Gosh! Did you have a bad accident?
First man : No. My son got his driver's licence.

190. *Boss to secretary* : Your typing has greatly improved – only six mistakes.
Secretary : O, thank you, sir.
Boss : Now let me read the second line.

191. Boss to new employee : I like men who are frank.
Employee : Too bad – my name is Joe.

192. Master to gardener : You lazy lout, why aren't you watering the plants?
Gardener : But it's raining so hard.
Master : So what? Take an umbrella and do your job.

193. Boss to future employee : You said you have two brothers – what do they do?
Future employee : O, one is in the jail, the other one in the hospital.
Boss : Good god, what happened? Did they have a fight?
Future employee : No sir. They work there.

194. *Servant to sleeping master :* Wake up! Wake up!
Drowsy master : Why are you waking me up?
Servant : You have to take your medicine for sleeping.

195. *Boss :* Why do you want to extend your leave?
Employee : O Sir, you know I got married two days back.
Now my wife wants to go for a honeymoon and wishes that
I should accompany her.

196. *Master :* You are dismissed as from today.
Servant : But why? I haven't done a thing.
Master : That's why.

197 "How many people are working in your department?"
"Counting the boss, 20."
"I see. Not counting the boss, is it 19?"
"Oh no. Without the boss, nobody works."

198. *Boss :* Why are you late for work today?
Employee : Because yesterday you said I should read the newspaper at home.

199. *Memo to boss :* With reference to my horoscope for today, please confirm the forecast pay raise!

200. Manager to secretary : I want to put up this notice in the office where everyone will see it.
Secretary : That's easy. Put it up near the wall clock.

201. Lady (interviewing servant) : Can you cook?
Servant : Yes Ma'am. Both ways.
Lady : What do you mean, both ways?
Servant : Whether you want the guests to come again or not.

202. Master : Why were you thrown out of your previous job?
Servant : Because I swatted a fly.
Master : Just because you swatted a fly?
Servant : Yes – it was sitting on the master's nose.

203. Proprietor : I am very happy with your work. I will promote you as manager and double your salary.
Employee : That won't be of much benefit to me. However, if you were to appoint me as cashier.....

204. Maid : Show me some consideration – I have worked for you for so many years – even my hair has turned white.
Mistress : Yes, of course. Here is a tenner. Go and buy yourself some hair dye.

205. Boss : What is your name?
Interviewee : Shall I tell you in Urdu, English or Hindi?
Boss : Tell me in all three languages.
Interviewee : Well, in Urdu it is 'Paigam', in English it is 'Message' and in Hindi it is 'Sandesh' Kumar.

206. Boss to new employee : Did the division chief assign any job to you?
New employee : Yes, he said as soon as you appear, I was to wake him up.

207. Employer : Why did you leave your previous job?
Servant : Due to frustration.
Employer : Why, what were you frustrated with?
Servant : O, I wasn't frustrated with anything. But everyone in the house was frustrated with me.

208. Boss to applicant : You have no experience at all. Yet you expect a fat salary.
Applicant : Just give it a thought, sir. Since I have no experience, won't it be that much more difficult for me to work?

209. Master shouting at servant : And don't you do anything without taking my permission first.
After a while, the servant comes.
He says : Master, there is a cat in the kitchen and it is drinking the milk. Do I have your permission to shoo it away?

210. Master to servant : Go and see what the time is.
Servant : I don't know how to read the time.
Master : OK. Then tell me where the small hand is and where the big hand is.
Servant (after a while) : Master, they are both inside the clock.

211. Boss to secretary : What kind of a report is this?
A report should be clear and simple, so that even a moron can understand it.
Secretary : O, I'm so sorry, sir. But which part of the report have you not understood?

212. Servant : I want to leave this job – you don't trust me at all.

Master : What do you mean by that? Even when I go out of town, I leave my bunch of keys on this table.

Servant : What's the use? Not a single one of those keys fits your locker!